fox

Jinny Johnson

MARSHALL PUBLISHING • LONDON

Rusty was born in an underground den. There, she and her brothers cuddled together to keep warm.

Now the cubs like to play outside. They are very curious and poke their noses into everything.

Look at Rusty's big ears. She can hear the smallest noises. If she is frightened, Rusty will run back into the den to keep safe.

Rusty looks for worms and beetles in the grass. When she is older, Rusty will learn how to catch mice and rabbits to eat.

Foxes will eat the food we throw away. Rusty has found some tasty scraps in a bin.